AN
EASIER
LIFE

changeitbooks.com

AN
EASIER
LIFE

Table of Contents

Thank You for Your Kindness

Barbara Durette

Heidi Winter

Dave Cannon

Fab Natale

and always
and every day

Constance and Zechariah

and

My Daughter Chloe

Introduction

What you do, what you stand for and what you contribute matters.

Life can be frustrating. It's easy to feel hopeless, powerless and insignificant. It can seem ridiculous to think you can have a positive effect on things that are important.

Each time you offer kindness you effectively change the world.
In the moment of choosing to be kind, generous, compassionate or humble you make a statement about believing there is a way to bring about positive change.

Kindness and caring are good for the one receiving, certainly for the one giving and inevitably for the whole world.

Part One

me, myself and i

All You Need Is...

I was taught that love is the solution to many problems. If we could learn to love each other the world would be a different, "better" place, and many of the struggles between individuals and groups would diminish. Even though the idea of a world full of love is exciting, our daily reality seems a long way from love catching on and becoming the force that will make the world a more livable place.

According to the songs, teaching, sayings, poems and what my religion taught me, we must love everyone. Love my neighbor; love those I don't know, even those who are my enemy. Much of the time I stumble when it comes to loving in the easy places. I mess up with my family, my friends and those I care for, so how do I love strangers and those I don't like?

I was taught love was something special and it lives in committed places, between lovers, partners, siblings, parents and children and maybe very close friends.

I understand that. Give me an important relationship, a great deal of time, allow me to develop trust, connection and a long history and then, love. That makes sense and seems "natural" to me.

There is no way for me and I imagine for you, to love the person you pass on the street, and those we have quarrels with or don't like. The thought is lovely but the reality is unrealistic.

This is one of the reasons we have a hard time getting along. If the basics are difficult to understand, how do we live a "better life"? How do we follow guidance that's so hard to make sense of?

I ran into James a few days ago. He was very excited.

I'm so happy. Cindy's pregnant! We're going to have a baby. I'm ecstatic, we've been trying for 7 years and now we finally have our wish.

After the initial excitement had passed, James lowered his voice and said,

I'm kind of scared. When I woke up this morning, and came back to earth, I got worried. I have no idea how to be a parent; I mean it's not like there's a manual. Right?

No manual on parenting, being a friend, a partner, a co-worker or a human being? Maybe it's not that complicated. Maybe it's not love at all.

We Undervalue Kindness

Sydney is a friend of mine. I've known her for years and the more I watch her and spend time with her, I'm certain Sydney understands life differently than anyone I know. Sydney never misses an opportunity to help others. She fills her pockets with change before she walks through the downtown streets. Sometimes she picks up other people's garbage, pleasantly speaks with strangers and offers acts of kindness to people whether she knows them or not.

I've been there when her phone rings or hums with a message. The person on the other end is asking for a favor or for Sydney's time, and every time she says, *"Sure, where do you want to meet? What do you need? No problem."*

For a long time, I thought Sydney must have an agenda but after years of watching and listening, I've come to realize it's who she is.

Sydney, I don't understand, why are you so available and interested in others? Why so caring and understanding?

Each time the response is the same and each time I'm surprised and look for the flaw and the reason why.

I respond because I'm able to. I help because I can. Every time I'm asked to help or give of my time, I realize I'm the lucky one. I can't think of anything greater for one human being than to be needed and to be able to respond to that need.

I'm no saint, but I know caring is better than not caring. I'm happy to be able to make any kind of difference.

I've seen people Sydney has helped, be mean to her.

I watch her grimace and I know when she's being used it hurts. Instead of expressing frustration, she says things like, "maybe tomorrow will be better" or "I hope they aren't bitter forever." Or get this, "I don't know what's going on in their life, maybe they're in a bad spot."

Sometimes Sydney gets a request from the same people who were mean to her only days before and she goes back, warm and welcoming, offering to make a difference. I get frustrated with her.

Sydney, don't let them hurt you; don't go back for more, what's wrong with you?

We all have choices and mine, when I'm able and strong enough, is to be kind. What are the alternatives? Should I add to the mean, selfish and inconsiderate in the world? I refuse to believe caring doesn't matter or make a difference. I won't say, oh well, or whatever or who cares. I benefit by offering myself and maybe it makes a difference that I wasn't too busy, apathetic or tired. Maybe it matters that I gave a damn.

6

My friend Sydney understands kindness and caring are good for the one receiving, certainly for the one giving and inevitably for the whole world.

Drop the Capital

The fundamental problem with how we relate to each other is "me first". I'm not familiar with how children are raised in other cultures, but it's not uncommon in the western world to be taught, "we're number one".

Until we can move from being first, from thinking of us and our needs and wants above others, the vicious cycles of mean, jealous, hurtful and hateful will continue.

I
I am
I need
I want
I'm entitled
I deserve
Me
Me first
Mine
My

The opposite of kind is more than mean, it's selfish and self-absorbed and as long as we teach, "we're number one", kindness, concern and caring for others on a large scale, will never be possible.

I remember a walk up a long flight of stairs several years ago. I was behind an older man of 60 or so. He was walking on the right-hand side, holding the handrail and slowly making his way to the top. I was five or six steps behind him moving at about the same pace. As he approached the last few steps, a woman arrived at the top of the stairs, coming the other way. She had a child of four or five years old with her.

The child began going down the stairs on the same side as the man. There was a brief moment of confusion as the child and the man arrived at almost the same place.

The man looked up at the mother who was still standing on the landing; his body language told me he was looking for something. I fully expected the woman to call the child and redirect him. Instead, she looked sternly at the man and said, "he's only a child, aren't you going to move and let him pass?"

The poor man moved to the left and allowed the child to push past. This child believed he was entitled to the man's space and he understood, if the man didn't move out of his way, his mother would fight for his entitlement on his deserving behalf.

How will this child ever come to care about others? How will he know of sharing and consideration? How will he learn about community and responsibility? How will he live in a world that desperately needs another approach?

We're number 1
We deserve.

10

We're entitled.

Only the strong survive.

It's a dog eat dog world.

These positions are about nothing but you. This is the fabric of despair and regret that lead to empty, lost and lonely. There are so many, "I wish I'd known", "I learned too late", "I 'accumulated' so much and leave with so little."

Mohammad is a man I've known for about two years. He is genuine and gentle and in the land he comes from or in the family where he was raised or both, he was taught his happiness and well-being are secondary to that of his guests. Mohammad would never consider his comfort or happiness first, nor would he tell you what he wants or needs because he wants you to be happy and comfortable.

His chair is yours, his money if you need some is yours; his bed, if you choose to spend the night is for you, because in this setting he doesn't know how to be number one. Mohammad is concerned more for your well-being than his own, and it's awkward to be around him because our training is so different.

At first, I caught myself thinking, "is this guy for real? There must be a catch". In time, when I learned to relax and let him follow his training, it was lovely and the atmosphere was ripe for mutual consideration.

It's remarkable to experience what it feels like to have another attend to your well-being.

"You honor me by allowing me to do for you", Mohammad once told me.

Imagine that.

It's this ability to question, "we must look after ourselves first", that will lead to a new way of thinking, acting and responding.

I recently moved into an apartment building. It's a different experience than living in a house. In many ways everyone in the building lives in the same house. If you never understood, we're somehow all connected and related, you get it quickly when you live in an apartment building. If you mess up the garbage disposal you mess it up for everyone, including you. If you break something it's broken for all. If you're loud others will hear. If you forget what you do matters to your neighbours, you may be reminded when you need them to remember you have needs.

In many ways apartment living is a wonderful, sometimes painful reminder that others must matter, because they have a physical connection to you. Even in this environment, the "I" surfaces and takes control. The "me" rules and the atmosphere is altered and everyone suffers.

Only yesterday I attended my first residents meeting. There were several items on the agenda; only one was of interest to me. A few days earlier the property manager had been replaced and many of us wanted to know why. In a short time, I'd come to know and like this woman, but something happened between her and I suspect the wrong person and she was gone.

In an instant her life was altered forever. She felt the wrath of the administration of the building and without warning, was without a job and maybe without a future.

It was interesting to watch the group of 50 or so be offered a story about something that didn't add up. Even with the holes and excuses, the majority moved from a position of "we want answers", to "oh well, I guess that's the way it is", and "that's good enough for me".

The details of the meeting and the problems in my building aren't important. What is important, is how quickly a group with some concern for another was swayed to "leave it alone". This group of people stayed with injustice, unfairness and the human cost to this person for a few minutes, but once fed a story that sounded official, were quickly off to talking about tree planting, elevator maintenance and power washing. And in only that much time they were content with worrying about themselves and their surroundings while the person in question slipped from sight. The concern had lasted a moment and when the tussle was over, whatever else mattered to the group surfaced.

The rule "if in doubt worry about yourself" seems too often to be the wisdom of today.

Let it matter what happens to each of us. Let us care enough to be involved.

I will save you as long as I don't have to get too involved.

I don't mind throwing you the rope but don't ask me to get wet.

I'm happy to give you a hand but how much did you say it will cost?

I'm a decent person concerned with others, but let's not go overboard.

"Are there any other issues that concern you tonight?" the chairperson asked. One by one the hands raised and the list was formed, one by one they forgot why they had come, or felt they had done their best; yet she still needed us. We were her hope. In fact, we may have needed her, more than she needed us.

I did my best.

I tried.

I showed up.

I asked the questions.

There are two types of kindness; one that's casual and can be done in passing and another that takes a greater effort and commitment. By holding the door for someone, you have offered some kindness. This isn't to be sneered at. It's a start and shows on some level you appreciate and understand we don't live in isolation and we survive as a connected group.

Allowing someone to come or go first, please or thank you, basic courtesy and consideration are little actions of intention that move us to a caring level of interaction.

Active kindness requires a commitment that says, "I care to the point of involvement."

Mohammad will give up his bed, his comfort and his needs for you and he feels lucky to have the opportunity.

I want to care that much too.

I will get wet to help you if you need me to get in the water.

I will get dirty if required and understand it is being in the dirt that enables my humanity.

I will risk standing out to be involved in caring for you.

Until we're ready to risk, to be uncomfortable and to matter where our efforts are concerned, committed kindness will be nothing more than a nice idea.

Have you ever wondered where some of our "rules" come from? Traditions passed from generation to generation often with little or no thought.

What of the rule that says, "we must capitalize the first letter in a person's name?" Maybe if we stopped ascribing so much attention to the "I" we might be prepared to look differently at the rest.

I need to consider and re-consider.

I must ask questions.

It's my responsibility to say wait, or why, or no, not any more.

I am an individual, unique but not special relative to the group.

I am an important part of the whole.

I understand I have a place and it's not necessarily at the front or the top.

I am happy to have responsibility to others and the world at large.

I am pleased to know I need to make a difference.

I am happy to drop the capital and all it may imply.

No Secret

I have been having morning coffee at the same coffee shop for more than a year. There is a woman who works behind the counter who seems unhappy.

I don't know if her apparent unhappiness is about her job or another part of her life but she is distant, disinterested and often quite unfriendly. If the line brings me to her service window, I am never sure what I'm going to be greeted with but it's never pleasant. I have watched this person respond to a number of customers with such indifference, I wonder if there have been altercations.

A few months ago, in mid-November, a man came to the coffee shop I had not seen before. He got the same treatment on a number of occasions that everyone else gets from this person. I probably wouldn't have noticed him but he arrives at pretty much the same time as me, so I have been able to watch the interactions.

Just before Christmas, I watched something amazing unfold. My fellow coffee drinker arrived shortly after me and when it came his turn to be served by "this person", he took a moment to address her.

"You're here a lot', he said. "Do they ever let you go home or do you sleep here too?"

She looked at him initially with a glare but as she studied his face, she could tell he was taking a moment to be interested in her.

She said something I couldn't hear but I heard him say to her, "I hope you get a little time off at Christmas."

Then he put out his hand and said, "my name is Richard, may I know your name?"

She paused for a moment, studied him further, could see he was sincere and reached out to shake his hand. "My name is Mary" she said, and she smiled faintly.

I have been in that coffee shop many times since that encounter between Mary and Richard and now I watch with fascination and hope, to see that every time he comes in, they exchange a few words and always a smile. Last week I saw her looking for him and when he arrived, her face grew softer and she waited cautiously and happily to serve him and spend a few seconds. I even heard her say one day, "you're late today, thought maybe you weren't comin."

Richard always smiles when he sees her, and each time he takes a moment to have a brief, personal interaction that seems to sooth Mary and makes both of them smile.

The secret to getting along is really no secret at all.

It's not love or anything that cumbersome or confusing. Love requires lengthy commitments and a lot of time. It also means we have a number of things to negotiate and sort out and then there's, do you love me too? Do you love me the way I love you? Will you love me forever? What exactly do you mean by love? What rules do we consider when establishing our love relationship? And so much more.

Basic kindness, an honest bit of attention and the act of respecting another, even in a passing moment, carry with them all that's needed to change our point of view and the way we relate to others.

Let me show you.

Where do You Want to go From Here?

Until we learn to care for ourselves and offer self-kindness, there's little chance of being able to offer caring or kindness to another. We can become so wrapped up in ourselves and the baggage we carry around with us, it affects everything we are.

By way of example, let me tell you about Diana. When she was a child, Diana was attacked by a stray dog. Today Diana is not only frightened of dogs, she's also cautious of people. Any new person or situation is viewed with distrust and fear to the point where it's difficult for Diana to connect on a meaningful level.

Diana and I came to know each other a few years ago. It was clear in a short time she was her dog attack. It affects her judgment and controls her feelings and possibilities.

"I was attacked when I was 8, and I needed stitches in my leg," she rolls up her pants. *"and on my arm"* she rolls up her sleeve, *"and even on my neck,"* I can see the scar.

In many ways, Diana is that ugly story. She tells it, lives it, and shows it and until she can put it in perspective, she will be controlled by it. Diana needs to put the horrible attack in her past as one of many events that have come to shape her. That part of her life was black but it needs be seen as a dark moment and not the defining moment. The only one who can do that is Diana but Diana and the painful event have developed a relationship. The dog attack has given her life definition. I know, easier said than done but Diana may want to try this:

I was attacked by a dog and dogs make me nervous. Since that day I have been cautious of many things. I want to understand all dogs don't want to hurt me and all of life is not to be feared and kept at a distance.

Diana's attack is only a part of her life's mosaic. Until she's kind to herself and able to put this event in perspective, she'll have trouble seeing the places, people and opportunities around her.

It's important to tell our stories, to speak of the past and to acknowledge where we come from. We need to understand what our history has done to us, how it has shaped us, and what gems and demons have attached themselves to us. Our stories need to be told, heard, acknowledged and sorted through. There's no way to move from a stuck position until we can say how we got there.

Only with a great deal of honesty and courage can we say, "This is who I am with my strengths and weaknesses, my plusses and minuses." Then you can decide what part of your past you want to identify with going forward and what part you want to see as something from yesterday.

Unlike Diana, many of us are pretty good at naming our skills and talents and expressing positive things about ourselves. That allows us to feel good about where we have been and hopeful about where we're going. Unfortunately, this "I'm doing great" posture may not be doing us any favors. If we only spend time on the "good things", we may be putting off looking at the whole picture.

It's important to appreciate the blend of our past experiences and the reality of our life story. Acknowledging who we are, where we have come from and what has shaped us is vitally important. Our history and stories, positive and negative are us. It's important to know yourself in all your "nakedness", own your stuff and move forward saying "from here I would like to try and go honestly, openly and new."

To say for instance, I'm a mean person, I understand I'm mean because of an event or series of events in my life is wonderful self-understanding and honesty. But to never use your insight to move forward from that place, is neither kind to you or those around you.

"Where do you want to go from here?" Or, "what do you want to do now?" are kind questions to ask someone who is stuck or in a low spot. They offer freedom and the opportunity to no longer be trapped in the story you were in yesterday. They offer the hope of something new.

I first met Nick three years ago.

I adored my wife. Being around her was all I wanted. I thought we were happy. Then there was the day I started going through her phone. I guess I shouldn't have done that but I did and I found there was another person. She destroyed my world. I've been unhappy and angry ever since.

I listened to Nick's story and eventually asked how long ago it had been since these events? Nick told me it had been 13 years. The power of what had happened many years ago still owned Nick and as a result anyone he encountered would come into contact with a man who was bitter and angry.

Find a way to do business with your painful past. Allow your hurt to become part of who you are and where you have been, don't let it be all you are and all you'll ever be.

Until you can let yourself off the hook that you and life have put you on, tell your stories as part of a bigger picture and not the only picture in your life, you cannot fully understand kindness.

Part Two

Making Life Easier

Come Closer

I sat with an old friend and we talked about the shape of the world. My friend has been a chef for many years and he is a quiet observer. What he said surprised me.

As far as I can tell, the biggest problem we face is a belief we need to look after "us" and not concern ourselves much about others. Whether I think about people who've worked for me or the countless people I've served, I'd have to say, very few have ever seemed to be interested in me.

I don't expect people to offer me anything. I'm happy to do what I do and hope the food I prepare meets with approval. But there's rarely a time I don't feel like the interaction has been about anything more than food, service and dollars and cents.

Maybe people don't want to get involved or be personal. I only know the feeling I have is that the people I have prepared food for, want what they want and besides that human interaction is brief, absent or phony.

If my friend is right, here are some things to consider when dealing with others.

To Be New

They say, first impressions are important because we only get one chance. Yet sadly, there is often no chance at all. Strangers are regularly treated with suspicion and contempt because they are new. In an instant we size them up, determine who they are, what they're about and what they're worth.

Each time we meet another we have an opportunity to begin again. Every casual contact gives us the chance to offer something never before tried, risked or imagined. Each passing of a clerk in a store, a ticket taker at the movies, the server in the restaurant, the teller at the bank, the person begging on the street; each person who buys from us or sells to us, allows us the chance to "do it differently".

Coming face to face with someone we have never seen before offers the chance to be completely unusual. We can, in that moment, be free to be the person we have wondered about being. We can leave our baggage and shortcomings behind and challenge all the "stuff" we carry with us.

It would be almost like saying, "Hi, my name is Joe. I used to be unfriendly, small minded and harsh. I have lived my life with it all figured out. I've been cold and distant, rarely making an effort. I have put people into categories based on what they looked like or whether they could do anything for me. But as of this moment, I realize that's been short sighted and full of hate. I realize this point of view has had everything to do with me, my upbringing and the beliefs and fears I bought into. I don't want to do that or be that person anymore."

Joe you see did it this way or that all his life. Joe was stuck, but as of this moment or maybe even for a moment he's going to slip out of his training and risk something new.

Susan is full of fear and loathing, the lenses she wears can only be worn in the brightest sun; they tint everything black. Susan has it all figured out and everybody is either up to something, owes her something, or needs to be distrusted.

Susan is angry! She sees and spreads hatred, suspicion and judgment wherever she goes. People are determined by their skin colour, religion, sexuality, age, facial features, hairstyle, clothing selection, bank account and who she imagines they are.

Susan hates and leads with contempt. Only those who she has learned to manipulate or gain from have any value to her. Sadly, Susan's not alone in her point of view.

One day I asked Susan why she was so bitter and unfriendly? Why so narrow and angry? She shook her head and called me naïve.

You don't get it! It's a dog eat dog world and until you get that you'll set yourself up to be disappointed and used. You're a fool looking to be taken advantage of. The world's a cold place where no one cares about you. Why should you care about them?

Susan's tirade was troubling, but more than that, she chose to lecture me in front of five others. I watched the room and the faces as Susan spoke. Her point of view had support. The others in the room nodded and agreed in their silent way.

These days Susan sits by herself. She's grown old, more bitter and certain the world deserves her response. Susan doesn't see many people anymore but her influence and point of view thrive. Susan never reached out and tried to make a positive difference. She only invested in more of the same and even though she's now alone, she's not by herself. Susan is everywhere.

Each time you encounter another you have the chance to set the tone. Each time you have some control of how that encounter will go because you are one of the participants. Each time you meet a person, be it for a moment or a relationship, you have the chance to be new. You can drag the ugly with you or leave it courageously behind. In that moment you hold your world in your hands.

I'm happy with who I am and how I act. I'm ok with my effort and with the way I think.

Or

Maybe I could think about things differently. Maybe I could be a little more open, giving and friendly. Maybe I could leave "the way it has been" at home and try something else.

Do it for you.

Do it so you can feel better with your presentation, so you can be selfless and gain from your kindness to another. Do it because you have a chance to be new every time you encounter someone else.

Try unexpected acts of kindness and see what that does for you.

Bring your hairdresser a cup of coffee.

Offer to get lunch for someone you work with.

Say something nice to a stranger with nothing more in mind than the compliment itself.

Give to someone who asks of you.

See how it feels.

Your act of caring, concern and kindness will hold a greater reward for you than the one receiving your care.

I have a chance with every encounter, and every person I meet to be brand new.

We Are Each Other

A skirmish breaks out on an airplane that's in flight. In moments the ruckus turns into an all-out fight and one of the people involved pulls out a gun and threatens to fire.

"Don't shoot", yells the flight attendant, *"if you pierce the fuselage the plane will depressurize and none of us will survive"*.

If you stop the story here, you might say to yourself, "he won't shoot, he must see if they die, he dies too." Apparently not, because we "open fire" every day. We don't seem to understand we're all on the "same plane" and everything that happens by "the worst of us" or to "the least of us" also happens to the rest of us.

Throw garbage on the street you damage the world for everyone including yourself. Diminish, demean or degrade another and you harm the entire species and the whole world suffers, including you. The starving are an appendage of our species. The injustice in the world is ours. The hatred, anger, violence and intolerance are all the problems of every one of us and they affect us as much as the bullet through the side of the plane involves all equally, including the person with the gun.

We are all connected and related. We have a common interest; our world and the betterment of our species.

Until we understand this, we're doomed to continue to "go down with the plane". Not only do we have to stop the shooter but we have to teach them that shooting hurts everyone.

Several months ago, I was in a fast food restaurant and not far from where I was standing an argument broke out between two women. One was a young person in control on the service side of the counter and the other was a much older customer who was only getting in deeper. It was clear these two couldn't communicate and things were on the verge of "out of control". The food store manager told the customer she wasn't going to change the order again.

The older woman said,

"I asked for x when I placed my order and it didn't come, I'm still asking for x and it still isn't here. What do I have to do to get what I want?"

The tone was heated and the volume was high.

At this point the manager took what was on the tray and said,

"I'm not serving you. You can't eat here. Get out."

The older woman stood there amazed; clearly shaken and hurt.

"I just came in to eat," she cried.

The manager dismissed her and walked away.

I continued to watch; the restaurant had more than a dozen people within feet of the exchange and yet there was no response by the bystanders.

From behind the crowd came a man who spoke quietly to the distressed woman. He took her by the arm to another part of the restaurant, sat her down, calmed her and asked what she wanted to eat. He returned to the counter and collected the order. The manager saw what was happening but did not intervene. He dropped off the food, made sure she was settled and left.

Whenever possible, offer peace, kindness, generosity and empathy.

There's no currency richer than a moment of kindness and caring. There's nothing to it and one day you or someone you care about will be the one in need. What was gained by a few caring minutes in the restaurant that day, offered a greater reward than what was received.

At every chance take a moment to offer something pleasant to those you come in contact with. Give them something to indicate that even in the few seconds you are engaged, it matters. Allow the other person to understand you're interested in them. Offer a pleasant comment to pass the time of day or a kind word to show you understand we're all on "the same plane." It's our social interaction that allows us warmth and connection and it's in that connection we thrive.

Be aware who's listening and watching. Your influence may be greater than you know.

Mark is a loud, pushy man, who likes altercation and feels it's his right to tell everyone who annoys him why and what they ought to do about their problem.

Mark has no trouble telling you how he feels about your wardrobe, you're driving, your choice of music or décor. He has no trouble commenting on anything about you that he finds distasteful or amusing. He does all this, claiming he's "just more honest" than most. Mark's maladjusted but he needs others to think his bad behaviour is about them. He doesn't have a problem with physical altercation either. If he has to use threats or push and shove someone who doesn't see his point, no problem.

I saw Mark last week. He spent time telling me his five-year-old son has been getting into trouble at school and he can't understand why. The boy is physical with the other children. He's loud and pushy and even told the teacher where she could go. You never know who's watching, listening and learning.

Be aware of the power of "the popular" and the media.

Many will be swayed by what they see on a screen. Television and The Internet while good for some things can be harmful when it comes to getting along. In many instances our screens have desensitized us and taught that certain attitudes and behaviours are acceptable. Often violence is portrayed as glamorous or sexy, and mean, harsh or inhumane are held up as things to aspire to.

It's difficult to argue with what society rewards and calls successful. We celebrate and admire mean characters and sensational violence. We get excited by horror, rage, anger and person against person behaviour. It's seductive and easy to be taken in. Unfortunately, these things have helped to create an environment for how we relate.

There's nothing hopeful about mean, arrogant, violent behaviour. The people who propagate hurtful and hateful either emotionally or physically do so because it feeds on our lowest common denominators. Those spots are easy to exploit, cause crowds to gather, group mentality to flourish and can be very profitable.

Resist the popular. Teach your children and those who look to you, "what's popular" is often about money and feeds the worst in us. Each time we're exposed to mean, violent or selfish we put another tear in the fabric of our world and provide a growing spot for something harmful.

It can be difficult to resist popular points of view. It takes courage, integrity and the ability to hold your own and stand against the crowd. From there, however, you'll get a good look at the value of kindness.

Mirrors

While there are countless mindsets and points of view when it comes to how we see the world and live our lives, there are a few that stand out.

The social or popular position, is hard to avoid and difficult to break free from. This is where we enjoy the approval of the group and where "what's popular" dictates our reasoning and actions. Here we live according to the mass mind and it's a dangerous place. We look to others to validate us and some will do almost anything to be needed or fit in.

Unfortunately, "the group" is powerful and is represented by society itself, and because of that it's difficult to challenge a person who lives here. They are after all, doing and thinking pretty much what most are thinking and doing. They dress, speak and act to gain points from the crowd and they're so caught up in what's popular, they're unable to see how their choices affect those around them and the world they live in.

There's a story about a famous thinker from the 1800's that speaks to the social layer. Soren Kierkegaard was a Danish philosopher who was so upset by "the popular point of view", he would go to the theater each time there was a new play, and he would, so the story goes, wait for what he felt was the appropriate moment, stand up and hurl his shoe at the stage and hobble out of the theater.

Kierkegaard was so convinced the popular media, (which was what the plays of the day were) was so infected with a lack of thought and integrity, he felt it his duty to protest what was being served as mind forming, cultural forming stuff. What he was saying by throwing his shoe at the stage was "this is garbage, see it for what it is, and think for yourself."

The image of Kierkegaard whipping his shoe at the actors, no doubt yelling something and then limping out with one shoe on and one shoe off has a comic side. Nevertheless, he made his point.

Rebecca is 13. She subscribes to many services that connect people. These "social places" give people a chance to share their thoughts, likes, dislikes, photos, dreams and even their daily routine. I imagine you know the kind of places I'm describing. Rebecca's pages were connected to many of the people she knew and also to a number of strangers. Not long ago Rebecca made an enemy. The story goes that Rebecca was getting attention from a boy who was also the desire of another girl at school. Unfortunately, the snubbed girl was popular and made it her business to use these "social pages" to do whatever damage she could to Rebecca. In only a few days Rebecca had lost many of her "network friends". She was mocked, bullied and had unkind and untrue stories told about her.

Within a week Rebecca wouldn't go to school. At two weeks she stopped eating and made a suicide attempt. Today Rebecca's family sit by her bedside hoping she will regain her desire to live.

Where was Kierkegaard and his shoe? Where was sanity and reason and where was the ability to escape the popular?

The social layer is easy to justify because it's everywhere and it's supported by "the crowd". Unfortunately, it shapes us and our world more than we might want to admit and it's no friend of kindness, hope, compassion and caring.

Claiming "human nature" is another popular life position. These are things about us that apparently come "naturally" and that we excuse as "just the way we are". They often include selfish, greedy and mean.

Every time we excuse our behaviour or attitude with "a shrug", we absolve ourselves of responsibility and the chance to learn and grow. By excusing some actions or attitudes by blaming "human nature", we let ourselves off the hook of honest self-reflection.

Jessie has a very good position with a large, powerful corporation and she enjoys telling friends or anyone who will listen to her gloating, how she clawed her way to a vice president's office. She revels in telling how she took advantage of every opportunity to be ruthless and self-serving. Recently, I had the misfortune of being at the same table as Jessie when she was going on about finding ways "to get ahead". There was a frightening consensus, that it was "good for Jessie". If she could find a way to move up, she should take it, "that after all, was "human nature".

The "I want to do it differently" point of view can be difficult to get to. It's tough to look in the mirror of your life and find places that need adjustment, improvement and change, and do what you know on some level you must. This is scary and requires honesty and commitment. It means leaving behind the popular and recognizing you don't want that anymore. You're no longer interested in gaining social points. The group's point of view has become tiresome and you need something more. You can and will think on your own and you are eager for the chance to try, even if it means falling.

Here you may lose friends and find yourself alone, but you'll go forward seeing life through new lenses. You might find much of what you counted on is worth less than you imagined. Leaving "the popular", may begin a road to integrity, honesty and new possibilities.

There are places and times in life that can become so painful, it's impossible to go on believing the same noise. If you're lucky you will arrive here.

> *I am a person responsible for my actions, my point of view and my life.*
>
> *I'm tired of excuses and telling myself the same lies.*
>
> *I can do better. I will do better.*
>
> *I have a responsibility for the world.*

My neighbor is all of humanity.

I have a responsibility for others.

I have a responsibility for the future.

I no longer believe everything I'm told.

I choose to be kind, caring and compassionate.

I want to be generous and giving.

I will no longer buy into points of view that allow me to diminish my humanity or the humanity of others.

I'm excited to make positive changes, regardless of the consequences.

What It Takes for Change

It takes women to change things for men, so men are no longer raised harshly, and expected to be what will hurt them and the world around them. When men are criticized or stereotyped may women stand with them in understanding and compassion, ready and willing to teach something more and show new options.

It takes men to change things for women so women are seen as partners and equals and no longer feel abandoned, dismissed or diminished. May the men assure their female friends they are eager to share and learn together.

It takes adults, parents to change things for children. New ways, new thoughts, new ideals are all the responsibility of adults, so tomorrow might be new. Children must be offered something beyond lip service. They need change that is loving, peaceful and kind.

It takes straight people to stand with those who are not straight until equality becomes a given. No more shall we be divided by love or the consensual expression of it. We shall only care that love is essential and be committed to it.

It takes my colour to change things for your colour and your colour to change things for mine until we no longer look for the differences but focus on the many things we have in common.

It takes my religion to change things for your religion and your religion to change things for mine until we forget the divisions. Risk, introduce something new and positive. Be tired of old feuds and many old points of view; they are good at continuing dead ends and hopelessness.

It takes "us" to stand with "them" until the lines are so blurred, we can no longer tell the difference. Work hard at not getting stuck on gender, sexuality, colour, religion, net worth and us and them. See what we have in common and forget our "man-made" differences.

It takes you to change things for me and me to change things for you. We don't need to make each other wrong. You can make it new for me and me for you. Together can we find something more.

It takes courage to risk, courage to be honest and courage to be new.

It takes understanding to see what we have and compassion to understand what we need.

It takes being tired of the same old broken mess to say, "no more, no way, not me anymore."

It takes the ability to risk, challenge, care and change inside and then excitement to look and see what you might offer outside.

Mostly though, positive change takes a commitment to being kind.

Acts

Much of this part of the book consists of ideas you may already know. Even though these suggestions are simple to the point of you saying, "everybody knows this stuff", they may be worth another look.

Try to make others feel included

See if you can help to create an environment where others feel encouraged to "become involved", and where they feel like who they are and what they say matters. In the same way a look or a comment can make someone feel unwanted, excluded and unimportant, so too can a word of acceptance and inclusion make a person feel worthwhile and welcome. A small indication from you to accept and involve another, can have an important effect on their life.

Allow silence in a conversation.

In our fast-moving world, we have forgotten the value of silence. Allow the chance to pause, reflect and consider. Ask for it if you need it.

"Could I consider that and get back to you?"

"I'm not sure, can we talk about this again tomorrow. I need time to think about it."

"Hold on, let me catch my breath. I need a minute."
Let the silence, the pause and taking time to consider, be as important as the words.

Celebrate the good things with as much time and energy as we give the negative.

Too often we rush through the positive and spend our time in the pain and the negative. This morning as I drove almost an hour in the car, I listened to a number of morning radio shows. Each one spent time speaking of a popular award show on TV the night before. Each station devoted a chunk of time "critiquing" the clothing, makeup and hairstyles of the women on TV the previous night. How many work places were filled with the same thing only a short time later? Bring a balance. A positive moment makes an important impact.

Compliment others

Risk. Be as sincere as you can be and offer something kind. It's not unusual to hear people being critical. Compliments or sincere attempts to make others feel good are rare. It takes courage to offer a compliment. Try it. You'll get to feel pleased you offered something nice and the person you were nice to will get to bask in the glow of receiving an unexpected gift.
"You made a great point during the conversation at lunch."
"Thank you for speaking up."
"I learned something from you today."

50

"I want you to know I consider you very brave."
"I'm happy to be your friend."
"I enjoy having coffee with you."
Even the physical, although potentially dicey, if honest and heartfelt can be warming and helpful to another.
"You have the whitest teeth."
"I like to hear you laugh, it's infectious and makes me feel happy."
"You look nice in that colour of blue."
We tend to hold our compliments close and hand them out with reserve. Let them fly, relish in the opportunity to help another feel good. Offer compliments easily, knowing you have the ability to be kind and generous and there is no cost to you.

Don't make others wrong.

There are times when we need to challenge what we have seen or heard. More of that would make the world a more responsible place. But so often in relationships, we aren't satisfied with how others present themselves and we need to "fix them". It's ok not to think the same and it's fine to come at a problem or a situation differently. It's in our differences where we learn and grow. Why do your choices have to be wrong if they aren't like mine? Why is it wrong for us all not to be the same? Most change and growth come from being exposed to new and different.

Try not being quick to determine the worth of others or the value of their point of view. If you must challenge, do so gently and with a desire to understand. Your conversations and disagreements will take on a new flavor.

Avoid should and shouldn't, right and wrong and good and bad.

These six words are responsible for so much misery. They tear at the fabric of our person; they keep us distant and divided and are responsible for all the human hardship history can show us.

Listen closely to a conversation, any conversation, your conversation. You may be surprised at how often we throw these words around. Unfortunately, it's so easy to move from individuals to groups and then before you know it, we're applying "our rules" to entire races, religions and nations. So many have been hurt by should and shouldn't, good and bad and right and wrong. Often a lifetime is needed to begin to undo the damage.

Amy told me she was forever scarred because of the small mindedness of others.

When I was a girl my mother left my father for another man. That kind of thing didn't happen in those days. I suffered judgment and ridicule. I was told my mother was a whore and as a result I was worthless. I can still remember all the hatred directed at me because my mother should have known better, it was all so wrong and I came from a bad family.

Both my parents are happy and they were miserable then. I wonder if their happiness would have happened if my mother had never risked. Everybody was so eager to live our lives for us.

Leave it alone, better still, notice the words, point them out and try to figure out what's going on.
My way is correct.
I know what you need better than you do.
Each time you're tempted to hurl should or shouldn't, right or wrong or good or bad, ask yourself why and what can be accomplished? Conversation and exploration lead to understanding, awareness and negotiation. Judgment, superiority and arrogance lead only to more of the same. Individuals and entire civilizations have been destroyed based on the sanctimony and criticism of others. Be careful with your judgement.

As they walk away

If the people who have just left us could hear what we're saying about them, would we be more careful with our words and more thoughtful about our easy ability to do harm?

Just be nice.

Nice is something each of us understands. What I need from you is exactly what you need of me. Without the ability to be kind we are lost.

Try:

A kind, warm word or gesture.

A pat on the back.

A kiss on the cheek.

An unexpected gift, at an unexpected time.

A compliment.

A genuine moment of eye contact.

An extra mile traveled happily.

Ask this of yourself,

What would that do to me and what would I like?

Any attempt to address these questions will benefit all relationships and make the way we relate very different.

The Kitchen Table

You might remember James who was expecting a child with his wife Cindy. After James yelled it from the rooftop, he calmed long enough to quietly confess he was scared. Being a parent is a daunting prospect.

"I just got worried. I have no idea how to be a parent; I mean it's not like there's a manual, right?"

Joshua is a warm and gentle boy. I know Joshua's mother; there's never a harsh word and never anything but grateful and happy for what she has. She's positive even in unhappy times and feels fortunate for what life hands out. She's the poster person for the cup half full. I know she hurts and at times wants, but the gratitude she echoes for her life and the joy with which she lives, are hard to be around without being humbled. There's never a task too great, a job too much, or a favor she isn't happy to comply with.

Joshua reflects it all.

He's young, stumbles at times and gets caught up in what it means to be an inexperienced teen. Generally, though, he's the loving, kind, caring person he sees in his mother. Ask his teachers, his friends and those who interact with him and they agree, Joshua is gentle, kind and aware of the needs of others.

I once asked Joshua's mother how she had managed to raise such a caring, considerate child? She smiled and said, "it's easy, Joshua reflects what he hears around the kitchen table".

With few exceptions, what children are shown is what they will reflect and in time become.

Nicole hates some kinds of music. She'll go as far as to have a tantrum when certain music plays on the radio. I've been in the car with her and her parents when a song comes on the radio she doesn't like. Nicole begins complaining and protesting to the point where the station is changed or everyone pays the price. I couldn't resist and asked, "What's with Nicole?" Sheepishly, her father admitted he and Nicole's mother aren't fans of some kinds of music and when Nicole was small, they would fuss and moan whenever a song was played, they didn't approve of.

Children generally reflect what they've been taught or have seen. There are some who learn by opposites and work hard to resist what they've been shown, but most simply copy.

We haven't protected our children by teaching them that many old attitudes need to be challenged. We have bathed them in the same shortcomings of yesterday. In many cases the mindsets and mistakes that have plagued us have been passed on to our children.

What we expose our children to will make an enormous impression on them and they will either become "it" or spend years trying to overcome "it". The time it takes to have a child and teach them to make a positive difference is all it takes for those of us who have children to change the world.

Parenting requires you put someone else first.

Being a parent means you understand there are others who completely depend on you. Ask yourself if you have what it takes to think of another before you think of yourself. That doesn't mean only "perfect people" ought to have children but it does mean, until you can say, "I understand the implications my attitudes and actions will have on my child," you may be unprepared.

Randi told me she did what was expected.

My mother pressured me. It was taken for granted I would find a man, get married and have a child or two. And it was assumed in the midst of that, we would buy a house, a car or two, get in debt and realize we had no idea what we were doing.

My mother, my sisters and really the whole society told me one way or another, these were the things expected and accepted. The baby screamed and we screamed at each other. It was horrible. Somehow, it's all planned and decided. There was something wrong if I didn't want the dreams girls are supposed to want. Before I could see I needed to grow up and figure out who I was, I already had one child and another on the way.

I wish my mother had said, 'it's difficult to be a parent. I made many mistakes. Let me tell you what I've learned and what I wish I knew then.' Instead she sold me a fairy tale she knew was false. What if she told me there was lots of time? What if she suggested I not marry young but take my time and grow up, what if?

Randi's story isn't uncommon.

What if we did it differently? What if we took the time to figure out "who we are and what we need" before we become partners and parents?

We marry and it's so often the same thing; long white dresses, long fancy cars, huge amounts of money spent on a show. Why the same thing over and over again with little variation and thought.

Each year the tree goes up, the decorations go on and the stores are busy. Each year we follow traditions with little thought for the message. And the critics moan about commercialism and missing the point and the cocktail parties are a buzz with how it's all gone wrong, but still there's no change.

The examples are endless.

We seem to somehow recognize, usually after the fact, that doing the same thing out of repetitive despair, leaves us empty and lost.

Children need us to have new ways of thinking. They need for us to stop wearing long white dresses and to get out of long fancy cars. They need us to question commercialism until it matters, and they need us to follow through. Children need us to consider what we say, how we say it and why. Mostly, they need us to care to the point of action and question to the point of deciding to make a difference. That means thinking, wondering and having the courage and insight to say no thank you, not like this.

Our children require us to stop and ask why, and when the why doesn't make sense or is simply the status quo, they need us to say wait or stop or no not me, not now, not like this. They need that before their birth and they need that same, "ask questions and find new answers", as we raise them.

Having children requires courage to be brave in the face of the socially expected so the next generation can thank their parents for more than technological accomplishments and the "accumulation of more". These thoughtful people will make a positive difference because they decided to risk.

Children need their parents to ask, "What are we doing and why are we doing it?"

My mother freely admits when she makes a mistake and teaches me how and why. We sit and talk about what just happened and we both learn and grow.

My parents taught me how to admit when I make a mistake. They showed me how to accept responsibility and not to feel shame.

My father taught me how to express my feelings in ways that don't involve yelling or hitting.

My parents make sure I'm kind, sensitive and caring towards others.

My mother shows me how to listen without interrupting or making harsh judgments.

My father taught me to share my things and myself. I know I'm not the most important person in my family or in the world.

My parents play with me and have taught me how to play with others.

When I was small my father played with me. We would sit on the floor and play games or go outside and play sports.

When I was small my mother taught me how to read and count with poems and songs. It was fun and we were together.

My parents taught me by showing me what events have to do with my feelings. They helped me understand what I say and do affects others and affects me too.

The list of wonderful possibilities is endless.

The "rulebooks" are written but they are difficult. They require adults take on the responsibility of raising their children with a wary eye to the popular and the past and with the intention of making a positive difference.

Let there be no more opportunity lost. Let kindness prevail.

Something Different

Having and raising children requires there must be changes to the way we relate, how we interact with each other and what we think is important. There must also be a change to the stories we tell each other, the stories we tell ourselves and what we offer to those in our care. It takes honesty to be a parent. It's important to know how to be honest with yourself; about yourself and about the world we live in.

Raising children takes men and women determined to communicate, negotiate and be open with each other. We must work in co-operation and respect each other in the process. I don't mean children need to be raised by men and women together but rather men and women must view and treat each other as gender groups differently, in order to create a new environment. Antagonism, aggression, suspicion, mistrust and many of yesterday's attitudes must be things of the past.

It takes courage to consider new options and possibilities. Yesterday's ways and choices need a close look to see what we need to hold tightly and what we must discard.

It takes the ability to accept that some of what we have is flawed and broken. And a desire to stand with the idea of change for the future so new ideas have a chance.

It takes a trash bin to throw out age-old stereotypes and images we have of what it means to raise a child. What children need, who they are and what we want to offer them needs to be reconsidered.

It takes brand new glasses as we look at roles and relationships. We must stop perpetuating the same lies and half-truths about how people relate and what's necessary for "success". Success has nothing to do with what you've accumulated and everything to do with the kind of person you are.

It takes wonder and commitment to tell children they are free to be whomever and whatever they might be. Not another copy of an old mold that has boys and girls believing they have to be this or that.

And it takes a good look at the whole picture, a wide-angle lens, to see even though things in your home or neighborhood might not look so bad, they're a mess in many spots. Inequity, injustice, unfairness and uneven distributions are all upheld, because we serve our children the same meal generation after generation. Children need to be told there are different options for them as individuals and a different future available for their world.

Mostly, it takes a commitment to kindness to let go of many of the things we cling to, kindness to see new possibilities and kindness in order to move our children forward to something different.

Do We Know Each Other?

Kindness is needed everywhere and yet it's elusive and rarely found to be consistent.

Until we can get "out of ourselves" and begin to consider others, we're certain to make the same mistakes as individuals and civilizations. As long as the "I", the "me" and the ego is in control, as long as we're motivated by "us first", humanity is hinged on a premise that is flawed.

The places where we need, maybe most of all, to forget the importance of "me" and what "I want and need" are the relationships that are closest to our hearts. Yet it's in these intimate, "sacred places" where we may need the most help.

We often have a difficult time being warm, concerned, compassionate and kind with those we have the deepest feelings for and the most to do with. We know from daily life that offering the ones closest to us what they need to flourish and feel cared for can be very difficult.

Over the next few pages you'll find some practical options for making close relationships work differently.

By close relationships I mean any place where you spend a great deal of time that's hinged on a loving commitment. It could be with children or close friends, but more likely this connection is a love relationship between those who have pledged love and commitment to you and you to them.

These are places where we can learn to offer and receive differently, that will teach us the value of kindness so we can feel it, live it and plant its seeds elsewhere.

The girl asked her mother, "Mother, how will I know when I'm in love?" The mother's answer wasn't very satisfying but true nonetheless, "You will know my dear, you will just know."

Kindness is the same, once you have offered it or been touched by it you will never forget and you may never be the same.

The Hard Part

It's difficult to say one part of establishing and maintaining a relationship is more important than another. Each piece that allows us to be with another is essential for it to all come together.

Close connections are complicated. There are though some important aspects to giving relationships of consequence the chance to work.

Changes and alterations can and must be made along the way but finding a workable starting point for an important connection is difficult. We come to relationships carrying so much of our stuff. Our stories and trappings come with us.

Start with honesty. There is a sense, where friends, possible lovers and even business associates are concerned, that we must lead with an image of what we imagine the other person wants.

I'm not suggesting you arrive at a first meeting and offer up your shortcomings and bad habits but don't provide something that isn't you in order to capture attention. A good opening impression mustn't come at the cost of a lie. Certainly, best foot forward and don't wear the clothes that have a stain on them, but don't offer "someone" to another who has little connection to the person you are.

I was having coffee with an old friend not long ago and she made a comment about "her work persona".

"Is your work persona different than the person who lives at home or spends time with friends?" I asked. She laughed, thinking I was being funny. "Yes of course, I'm different depending on the situation. The people, place and expectation all determine how I act and what I bring.

My friend may have found the root of the problem. Be consistent. Those around you will appreciate your honesty and in time come to trust you are what you claim. Even though, whatever you are and whatever you bring may need some work, it's at least an honest starting point.

Don't hide, lie or pretend where your insides are concerned. In time you will fool no one and be left to look disingenuous. Mirroring what you think others want from you, may leave you empty, lost and lonely.

You can either "be yourself " and decide, whoever that is, is fine, or you can be honest (this is much more difficult) and say, "now I've begun to have some insight into myself, my strengths and weaknesses, my needs, wants and shortcomings, I need to make some adjustments."

Deciding who you are and where you see yourself going is the first step to learning how to be in any relationship. This is difficult. We're so inundated by the media, our friends, families, education and religious background, being able to recognize our core, let alone deal with it, is an enormous task.

There's also that popular point of view that says, "love yourself, you're great the way you are." Hardly a recipe for honest, self-evaluation and growth.

If, however, you want to learn how to relate to others, as a parent, friend or partner, you must sooner or later look in the mirror of your life and say, "here I am with all my flaws and the stuff I carry around with me". After a close, hard look, you can walk away declaring yourself to be okay, or you can do business with what you see.

A healthy starting point might be, "I'm going to keep some qualities because I can't move on them or I like them. I'm going to rid myself of other parts of me, because they are unacceptable. I'm at a point where I can see some things need to go".

I have known Jana for about three years. She doesn't like her life, her relationships or where she sees herself going. We often talk about doing things differently. On this day Jana was beside herself.

I'm 30 years old and I realize I don't understand my feelings. I still have tantrums when things don't go my way. I dress like the people on TV because I want to be popular but I know it's all phony. My husband and I don't know how to speak, how to hear or how to relate as adults. We're stuck.

I told two of my friends this stuff yesterday; they looked at me like I had 4 heads. Are you kidding me? We're all so much a product of products. I want to learn how to be something more.

I will leave Jana with you. Keep her in mind as we look at some of the "practical stuff" to being in meaningful relationships.

Self-reflection and recognition are huge and ought to take a lifetime.

Let your life be a work forever in progress.

The Environment

The environment is about more than the level of the sea or the air we breathe.

The environment you create or help to create when dealing with others is essential to forming and managing a relationship that will work long term. The environment, along with "learn who you are and be honest about yourself", are essential to having a relationship.

Create an environment of trust and make sure the trust is real and dependable.

Those you relate to will need to know what happens in your time together is safe. They must understand you won't betray them, speak of their fears, shortcomings or weaknesses outside the bounds of your relationship, or without their permission. They need to know you won't use their "insides" against them.

"We are friends today but I may hurt you with the information you share with me" is out of bounds and even its possibility will never allow trust to exist. Those close to you, must know you will not "offer them up" in times of trouble.

Clive remembers his marriage sadly,

She would get angry and when she got angry, she would be mean. Things she knew I was sensitive about were used as weapons in moments of anger. My fears and weaknesses were fair game when she was upset with me. We went for counseling but I could never trust her. We divorced after six years.

What about this?

I'm honored to come to know you, to journey with you, to learn from you, with you and about you.

I will share with you and place my well-being in your hands. No matter where life takes us, we will remember where we began and where we have been.

In difficult or angry times, we will respect our history together and not exploit each other's pain, weakness or vulnerability.

If life moves us apart, we will remain conscious of our past and use kindness as our guide.

Anything you offer here is accepted in the spirit of our open, caring relationship. I encourage you to bring me your fears, dreams and fantasies. I will offer you the same.

I may question you for clarity or so I can learn, stretch and sort, but I will not judge you, make you ashamed or embarrassed.

If our dreams and visions become incompatible, I will either declare I can no longer keep up with you and ask that you help me to catch up, or I will ask you to go on without me.

I will never treat you with malice, nor will I forget the bond that unites us today.

Allow me, as I will allow you, to ask questions and pause for clarification, but never accept me being small minded or limiting in your dreams or quest for inner peace and happiness.

My ability to trust you will allow me to give freely. I hope to be able to gain your trust in return.

I will not tell you what you ought to be or how you must see the world. Rather, I will be excited to figure it out together with as open a mind and heart as I can.

When I get lost, angry, scared or petty, I ask that you help me. Remind me where we have been and what lies ahead. My need of your support and guidance will be a regular thing.

Create a space each day to offer to each other.

Life is hectic and often very busy. Don't let "busy" be an excuse for falling away from those you care about. Find a time every day, at most every couple of days to come together to hear and be heard. Create a place, where you can take a few minutes to speak and be spoken to. We make time for so many things; a moment or two to hear those we care for is essential.

Listen and be listened to.

Offer each other a negotiated few minutes to speak. In that time stay quiet and give your undivided attention. Allow this time to be free of judgment. Give freedom to the other person to tell you what's on their mind and only respond when their time is done.

This isn't speech time but a safe place for each of you to open up and be heard. The job of the speaker is to speak honestly about whatever's on their mind. The job of the listener is to listen openly and carefully to what's coming your way.

Offer empathy and if needed sympathy and when the speaking is done, let them know you heard them. This process can be healing and cleansing. So seldom does anyone give us a real few minutes where they stay quiet and listen. Remember, this is a trusting and trustworthy place. A place where you can be yourself, where you can say what you need to and be accepted and cared for.

This isn't the place to drop a bomb or name an important issue that needs to be dealt with in detail. These few minutes allow a time to vent, express and let go without the fear of something unwanted coming back. Usually, it's looking after the business of the day and life "as it happens". If something comes out of this time that needs more attention, negotiate a time to address it, but keep this space simple.

Learn to listen.

This is more difficult than it sounds.

Try to clear your mind of the noise that clatters around in your head.

Don't come into a conversation with your mind already made up. Listen to what the other person is saying. The ability to learn, grow, change and develop is key to a working relationship and dependent on being able to listen.

Try not to think of a response to what you're hearing.

Try not to feel you need to figure it out.

Try not to daydream or drift off following something the other person says.

Be careful of telling your story as you listen. Sometimes sharing a similar experience allows the other person to know you have empathy for them and understanding of what they may be feeling. Often though, "me too" shows you've somehow made their time and words about you. Remember, listening is about the other person; you will get your chance.

Focus and pay close attention, not only to the words but also to the emotions the other person may be expressing. Emotions are sometimes obvious; at other times you might have to watch carefully.

Resonate with the person speaking. Let them know you're with them and you heard them.

-You seem upset.

-This is important to you.

-I couldn't help but notice you were wringing your hands when you were speaking, is there more to this for you?

Remember, telling something important to another is among the most intimate acts a person can involve themselves in. Try hard to respect that and offer the attention and kindness these moments deserve. Sometimes just a nod, a note of assurance or acceptance may be all that's needed to encourage the speaker to go on.

Don't be afraid of silence, make use of it. Silence is an important part of this process. Consider what you heard and felt and then pause before you think about responding or defending.

When those close to you are telling you something important, try to feel and hear what's being offered. Are they conveying more than the words indicate? Is there learning here for you?

These are the moments when a relationship is tested and they only come along occasionally. Your ability to recognize something potentially important is happening, will make a difference going forward.

At the end of the few minutes the person speaking will likely feel heard and cared for. As the listener you will feel like you have enabled another to unload and be touched.

Remember, this is difficult stuff. Practice makes it easier. Try to listen over and over again. You'll make progress and you will be forging an important connection between you and the speaker, then the listener and you.

Open, honest and vulnerable.

Be direct; risk what's on your mind. Be open and honest but never cruel. Your friend or lover, your child or partner, will come to appreciate your candor and risk. It can be difficult to deal with those who aren't honest, and lying takes place in relationships in many ways.

> Fudging the truth is a lie.
> Not being fully expressed is a lie.
> Not following through is a lie.
> Being undependable is a lie and lies lead to
> mistrust and disintegrate relationships.
> It's much better to try and fall, then to
> pretend, hide or never try at all.

I knew a man years ago that thought he might be attracted to other men but he couldn't speak to his wife about his feelings. He worried about her reaction and whether she would be able to hear him. Eventually the marriage fell apart; not because he shared his worries and feelings but because he couldn't bring himself to risk and trust.

They had created a world where on this topic at least, honesty was out of the question. They lived their lives according to a model of marriage that had little room for human struggles. Him coming to terms with his sexuality wasn't the larger issue. The trouble was that risk and sharing was so difficult. The consequences of not being "okay" were greater than the opportunity to grow together in honesty and communication. He needed to be frank and speak his peace, not in belligerence or defense, but in openness and honesty. He needed to be able to share with her, and in his risk, they may have grown together.

It's important when you speak, you don't use riddles or play games. Say what you have to as clearly and easily as possible.

Don't renege on a promise.

Don't offer something and not follow through.

Don't pretend.

Don't beat around the bush for a lack of courage.

Don't fail to be honest and open.

Don't pay lip service to this stuff. You'll be found out. There are no imposters here.

Don't let those down who depend on you.

How about this?

Everything you do, do with an open, gentle, kind heart.

There's no place for hard, harsh and mean. We have seen and continue to see what a hard heart and a severe approach does. Let that be finished and let its end begin at home with those you care for. Let gentleness and kindness guide your actions and your disposition.

Try it with those you care about. If you can offer kindness, compassion, sympathy and empathy to those closest to you, where so much is invested, it ought to be easy to give it to strangers.

Bring warmth to your loved ones.

Allow them the room to grow and fall.

Encourage them to risk.

Provide them a safety net as they explore, change and learn.

Reassure them as they fall short.

Listen to them and let them know you heard and you understand.

Hold their hands as they wonder and assure them you will stay close.

Teach them how to break free of convention and stay with them as they try.

Your kind gentle spirit and heart will set the tone for your every interaction.

Trying It On

Try these with your friends or your partner, with those you work with and your children. See if they make a difference.

But first:

You must approach all of this, with a disposition to learn and be open.

If you have no time to consider new or different you will never succeed here. You must want to relate to others differently and be able to see the need for something new.

Everything here is based on the desire to get along and the need to understand how to do that differently than you have done it up until now. All of this lives under the umbrella of kindness. If you see the value of kindness and recognize the damage and dysfunction in the world, then you have the tools and point of view needed to move forward.

Start here.

Blame is a way to distance you from others. Take responsibility, even when at times the responsibility may not be yours.

We're often quick to blame and point out flaws and imperfections in others. It's easy to blame and difficult to accept responsibility.

Try this.

I'm an adult and I want whenever possible to take responsibility for my actions, attitude and behaviour.

I want to be big enough and kind enough to sometimes take your responsibility too. I believe kindness is never wasted.

I will learn to own the things I say and do and even the things I project or cause.

I will speak up when required and do what I can to make the world and those around me happier.

I will learn to pay attention because I have so much to learn and more I need to offer.

I will stop being a "storyteller" and an excuse maker. Instead, I will enjoy learning who I am and what makes me tick. I will seek to enable others with kindness and understanding.

Teach me, and be open to be taught by me. Let's learn together.

Try not to let your relationships become stale. When you have a concern express it but do so with gentleness and caring. It's in these exchanges where we test the mettle of our relationships.

Try not to make others wrong and you right. Instead, see what you have to offer each other. If for instance you say, "Honey, your nail biting drives me crazy". You're likely to get a response in kind. "Yeah, well you constantly playing with your hair is no picnic either."

If on the other hand you say, "I know habits, preferences and points of view are difficult to address and even harder to change. I know, I have many things I'm pretty stuck on. Could we talk about some of our habits? Maybe we can help each other."

If you get permission to pursue the conversation, follow that with, "I care for you and I worry about your nail biting, I don't want you to get sick and it looks like you're nervous. Is there anything I can do to help"?

Then ask the question, "Do I have habits that worry or bother you?" Your concern for how they appear, the message they may be sending and their health, not to mention the underlying affect their behaviour is having on you, will allow the conversation to get off on the right foot. More than that, your willingness to own you're not perfect, that you want to learn, grow and change too, will be motivation and inspiration for a new approach.

Imagine relationships where we're happy to speak of our flaws and shortcomings. Imagine where we relish the opportunity to hear the points of view of others and consider them with an open mind. That's not to say it's all up for grabs. It's ok to say, "on some points I'm unlikely to budge but in many areas I'm open to listen and learn."

You might ask, "Will you do this with me?"

Your presentation makes all the difference.

"How you say it" is everything.

Be genuine, and offer in the sincerest way, an effort to understand.

If you say for instance,

"I don't understand you, you're not making sense". You'll lose the other person.

If on the other hand you say,

"I'm sorry, I'm having trouble following you. Could you please try to have me understand what you're saying another way? It's important to me to see your point." You'll encourage another attempt and foster a feeling of warmth. You said the same thing, but the presentation was so different, the result will be unexpected.

"I don't understand", works much better than, "you don't know how to express yourself."

The way you present makes all the difference.

People in partnership relationships must be on equal footing.

If there's an imbalance of power in a partnership, or a fear of punishment, honesty is at stake. There is a difference in power between parents and children. But even here, if there can never be a time when there can be a coming together in openness, there may never be a chance for real understanding.

Parents and some partners must give up their power difference if honest communication is desired. If you insist on being "in charge", don't expect honesty. Try putting away your need to dominate or control and see how others respond to you. It's impossible to get honest, open communication from someone who's frightened of you and who worries about consequences. Give up control and talk to your friend, child, spouse, co-worker or employee. In time when they begin to trust their contribution matters, they will likely offer up honesty.

Until you're ready to be an equal player in a relationship, a relationship of quality isn't possible. Even with your children, talk with them, listen and explore with them. Allow them to know, even though you're the parent, you're not perfect and you struggle to find your way too. Allow them to see your humanity.

A true conversation will be full of possibilities and have all participants contributing while respecting and learning from the position of others. This doesn't happen overnight and if you receive information you don't like, say so, but say it with care, concern and a desire to learn. In time, the one with less power might begin to trust the environment is safe, and things will slowly change. Parents, this doesn't mean you become your child's friend. But it does mean an honest exchange where you might begin to hear and understand each other is possible.

Be prepared to say you were wrong, or sorry. Your open hand will gain you much more than your closed fist.

It's impossible to have a "relationship of quality" with someone who's usually right or often angry. Be able to admit fault, enjoy learning from those around you and see how it feels to say, "I don't know", "I'm not sure." What do you think?"

Ian admits to spending much of his life angry.

I was forever ready to argue and prove others wrong. I never backed down and I was certain everybody else was a fool. I didn't realize it but people were tired of me. One day I heard two of my friends talking. 'Whatever you do, don't get Ian going, he's always angry and ready to fight.'

That was an eye opener. I didn't want to be angry forever. It took people a long time to adjust, but they began to see I wanted to be open and less aggressive. It was important to learn to laugh at myself and not take myself so seriously. Once I learned how to do that the rest was easier."

Your ability to listen, to remain quiet and open, to be understanding, compassionate and humble will garner you some inner peace. It will also have others respond differently to you. Change and trust don't happen instantly but in time and with hard work both are possible. Set goals with your family or friends and ask them to nudge you when you begin to "go off". Tell them you're trying to make changes, ask for their help.

"I've been doing some soul searching and I can see there are some issues in my life I'd like to work on. I'd be grateful if you could offer me a bit of help in my effort to do things differently. I want to look at some new options for my life and my approach."

This will scare some and be attractive to others. Don't be surprised if you gain some new relationships and lose some old ones.

Mouth and ears.

It sounds odd but these two body parts and all they're "attached to" are at the root of so many misunderstandings and communication breakdowns. If we can remember our backgrounds, perspective, filters and "training" are vastly different than every other person, we'll have a chance to laugh at ourselves and be vulnerable. From here communication and honest relationships are possible.

At the beginning of a relationship you can never check and re-check too much. There are bound to be snags that need clarification. Even the simple things can get confusing. I ask you if you'd like to have a cup of coffee and you think any one of a thousand things. Unless one of us, or both of us are able to clarify, then I may be thinking, "maybe I have a new friend here" and you may be thinking, "Is this person coming on to me?" And with every example this kind of thing happens. What comes out of a person's mouth has to go through an uncountable number of filters before it settles in the other person's brain and you can be sure, some of those filters will "get it wrong".

Life is complicated and often difficult and our training is varied. Try to break free of your past and ask for clarification. There's almost a guarantee what you think you said or what you think you heard will somehow be different than what the other intended or went away with.

"But you said."

"But you did."

"But I thought."

Clarity and explanation will save you a great deal of confusion and pain. Being clear is an act of kindness and will allow you to get to know those you relate to.

Jack and Jill are on a date. Jill invites Jack to her home for dinner. Jack says to Jill,

"I loved the food you prepared tonight."

Jill is overjoyed and decides to prepare that same meal on a regular basis because it pleases her new friend. Unfortunately, Jack comes from a background where it's more important to compliment the host than to say how you feel and risk causing hurt.

Jack and Jill have a problem.

Relationships are like that.

The distance from your mouth to my ears and my mouth to your ears is so vast there is no way we can truly relate unless we risk and are honest.

Imagine a relationship where we commit to struggling to figure it out. Imagine finding that fun or exciting. I can never understand you or you me unless we help each other. If we make each other guess we will get it wrong and the consequences will be dire. It's in these moments of helping and struggling that we can understand and acknowledge who we are, where we come from and how we can adjust and adapt.

Your mouth and ears, based on where they have been and what they have been taught will need help. Try not to let things like pride and stubbornness, fear and an inability to risk, get in the way of learning how to get along.

Be kind and understanding and laugh at who we are and what we carry around with us.

Watch what happens from there.

Life is Difficult

Being in any meaningful relationship is difficult.
Where do we begin?
How do we relate?
What do we expect?
What do we offer?
How do we posture?
How do we make progress and make our relationship work, are all questions that cause us concern?

It's the opening attitude we carry with us that makes the difference. Check and re-check your attitude and your point of view and be honest with yourself.

This is the, "I'm completely naked and know exactly what I'm looking at" stuff. Once you find the courage to be honest about you, then you can begin to ask some of the essential questions.

What makes me tick?
Who am I?
Am I ok or are adjustments and changes needed?
Are my relationships great or could they use some work?
Is the world I live in doing fine or does it need some help, maybe my help?

If you're even a little bit honest, all of these questions will likely raise concerns for you, about you, your relationships and the world at large. Living in the world and relating to others is difficult. Openness and a willingness to learn and grow are essential. But it's tough to give up things that are familiar and hard to move to something new.

YOUR GUIDING PRINCIPLES AND ATTITUDES ARE EVERYTHING.

Desire change, look for new and different.

Seek internal change in your life and growth in your relationships. Look for these things in the world and in those you encounter.

The status quo in many ways is bent and broken and has shown itself to be disinterested in justice, fairness, equality, peace and betterment. Beware of "the way it is" or "the way it should be" or "this is how we do it here". These formulas usually represent points of view that are less desirable for most. They work best for the few who stand to lose the most if real change happens.

Seek to be honest, struggle to communicate and negotiate.

If you can make peace with this, you will have gained a great deal. This will move you from, "the world revolves around me", to understanding we're all related. This position inspires communication and understanding and looks for places where we can be happy together. A desire to negotiate brings us to the possibility of building a new tomorrow.

Be as generous as you can be, on as many levels as you can imagine.

Be generous with your time, compliments, patience and resources. Offer wherever you're able because there are others watching, listening, needing and being directly affected by your actions, words and attitudes.

Never miss an opportunity to be kind.

Kindness means more than being nice. It also means resisting things that are contrary to being kind and it requires that you consider the situation and do what you can to bring something helpful and hopeful.

Just today I saw a man in his 60's or 70's and a woman of maybe 20 being harsh with employees in stores where I was shopping. Anger, belligerence and entitlement damage the encounter. The typical non-caring "relationship" that often exists between strangers, takes away the opportunity for something more. An "I couldn't care less" attitude, continues what we have, and injures all of us.

If you don't like the encounter you find yourself in, do what you can to move things in a positive direction. Try being the person on the other side. Exercise your humanity. How can we find a solution? What can I do to make this easier? How can I respond in a way that enables things to be resolved in a peaceful, thoughtful way?

Do at least 51% of the work in any relationship.

Don't leave it behind for others to pick up after you. Don't think that less than "more than your share" will ever make things better.

Imagine relationships, be they at the most intimate level between partners, at work with co-workers, at home with parents and children or in the world between strangers, being tackled with each participant wanting to make a contribution.

Imagine being happy to help, keen to do for others and eager to take that effort and attitude with you everywhere. Consider for a moment a relationship, between partners, where each one wants to do for the other. Whether the doing consists of physical things like household chores, or emotional things like gentleness, patience and caring.

"I want to do more for this relationship." Imagine that being the mindset for all relationships.

I am not your keeper but I have a responsibility for your happiness and well-being.

There's a direct connection between you wanting others to be happy and them feeling that way. You are not an entertainment committee or tag along therapist, but you wanting others to make progress and enjoy life, are responsibilities each of us must take seriously.

We're not here to deter or determine the happiness of others. We must do all we can so those we love, those we know and those we encounter feel cared for, helped and encouraged. In other words, every person you come in contact with is in need of something from you. In some cases, they're in need of many things you can and need to provide. In many cases very little is required. A personal commitment from you to each person you interact with sounds huge but it's not. It's just an important investment in the future.

Make each connection count.

As I hold the door I do so with a smile because I'm happy to be of assistance.

As I tip the server it pleases me because I feel fortunate to offer some of what I have.

As I walk to meet my friend in the rain, I feel excited, because the connection is important and the effort is worth the relationship.

As I pledge to be a friend, parent, or partner, I do so with excitement. I hope my commitment will bring the chance to do better, to make others happy and to live life with the things gathered from our relationship.

Some will read this and scoff or feel cynical but this is it. It happens in the moment of commitment and choice to live differently and to make tomorrow free of things like guilt, fear and manipulation.

From here I make my choices based in kindness.

The Alternative

A story worth repeating.

All of the King's subjects know that hunting on the King's land is strictly forbidden. Nevertheless, food is scarce and so people put themselves at risk and go into the forest in search of something to eat.

On this day, a man is lucky to have been able to kill a young deer with his bow. As he walks back home with the animal slung over his shoulder, he hears the sound of horses coming behind him. Pretending not to notice, he hurries on his way. Not long after, a voice booms behind him.

"Hey you! Stop!"

The man with the deer continues to walk, a little quicker now. He ignores the call.

The voice comes again, only this time more urgent and angrier.

"You! Stop!"

The man comes to a halt and turns to face the sheriff himself.

"Yes sir", he says meekly.

"What are you doing?" asks the sheriff, clearly very angry.

"Doing sir? I'm only out for a walk."

"A walk!" Yells the sheriff.

"You've been hunting!"

"Hunting, no sir, everyone knows hunting on the king's land is forbidden."

The sheriff is enraged, "what's that over your shoulder then?"

The man turns his head slowly, sees the deer, screams in disbelief and drops the animal.

"I have no idea how that got there", he says.

We're not good at taking responsibility. We don't like to assume it as individuals or as groups. There are a thousand excuses and it's never our fault or our doing. Somehow, we were victimized or in the wrong place at the wrong time. Usually, it's about him or her or them.

The dog ate my homework.

The bus was late.

The rain made it tough.

The tire was flat.

The battery was dead.

My mother had a pain, my kids are a pain, my life is a pain.

Don't ask me, don't look at me, I'm just a bystander. I didn't do it; I have no idea.

Every issue we face when it comes to mean, aggressive, self-centered behaviour, either socially or personally, is our responsibility and can be altered by us.

Mean and aggressive get a great deal of attention today. The police worry about bullying and are apparently watching for it. Schools have policies where aggressive behaviour and picking on others is concerned. There are zero tolerance rules and they say everyone is paying attention.

Politicians love to speak of the bullying problem. It's trendy and their lip service makes them popular, especially with people who have school age children.

More and more it seems, there's another story about a young person who couldn't take the vicious treatment anymore and ended the misery by taking their life. Then the Internet's a buzz and all the right people say all the right things. Nevertheless, the problem persists and the aggressive, mean activity of the "pushy", angry person, victimizing the "weak", passive, or peaceful person goes on. And we're shocked and surprised, and we wring our hands and wonder why.

We speak of bullying and mean behaviour as though they're isolated problems that take place exclusively in school playgrounds, on social media pages or high school hallways. This is the problem, and until we come to terms with the root cause of ugly, angry and mean we're doomed to miss the point. We've become good at finding another reason or excuse. There are so many answers as to why this is isolated, makes no sense and has nothing to do with us.

We live in a society and a world that's pushy, angry and violent. Many young people can't wait to get their hands on the latest attitude-shaping video games that are built on aggression. We fill movie theaters when the content is brutal and we celebrate those with vicious attitudes and points of view.

There's a new kind of politician who paint themselves as "truth tellers" and people who "tell it like it is", but that's just a cover so they can be mean, cruel, divisive and self-serving.

Some "stars" and "role models", all in the name of profit, align themselves with vanity and selfishness. What they do make the pages of the Internet and is all over social media and we can't wait to roll in it and share it at lightning speed.

Some athletes who are "God-like", surround us with arrogance, ego and attitudes we wouldn't tolerate from other sources, but in the uniform of our team they can do no wrong.

We watch the pushy rise to the "top of their game" and it goes unchallenged. We patronize games where the strong "beat" the weak and say, "it's just part of the sport."

We watch television shows that pit person against person and we bathe in the warmth that mean and aggressive bring with it. We popularize nasty reality shows that demonstrate selfish, hurtful characteristics and the stars become social role models.

Our children carry devices that access "everything", and with that freedom comes so many possibilities, often filled with hopeless, brutal and senseless. As a child I was sheltered from the pain of dealing with death and I was never allowed to come to any kind of understanding around sex or sexuality or the facets and complications of future relationships that awaited me. I needed to be protected from those "adult things." But a broken nose while playing baseball or a cracked bone in my foot while playing hockey were worn as badges of honor.

I attended wrestling matches with my father where people seemed to be hurt and I watched the spectators. I attended hockey matches with both parents and heard the crowd roar more over a fight than a goal. The message was clear, the table was set.

We're involved in a love affair with the root of our problems and yet we claim not to understand. Where does the mean come from, where does aggressive, selfish and angry get its food?

The opposite of kind isn't only mean, it's self-centered, selfish and self-absorbed. "What I want and what I need" get a lot of attention. As a result, the bully is everywhere. We allow it, care for it and raise it to be stronger.

Partners are often mean to each other, using threats and manipulation as a tool in their relationship.

Teachers can be mean to students and sometimes need to be closely watched.

Coworkers can be horrible to each other.

Employers can subject employees to misery and sometimes the opposite is true.

Some police use their "special status" to break the rules and politicians push us around with lies, false hope, hubris and ugly bravado.

Wherever there's an imbalance of power between individuals or groups there's a risk of exploitation. Mean and selfish live and thrive in so many everyday places.

As long as we won't see the deer on our shoulder, as long as we can point to him or her or them and as long as we claim not to see or understand, the hurt and damage will grow and thrive.

The problem isn't that mean, selfish, ego driven behaviour is so prominent; the problem is there is no real alternative. Only when we can point to something else as desirable will we have an option.

Consider for a moment some of the giants in our society. The fashion, fitness and beauty industries for instance, are enormous in their influence. Walk into a department store or a mall, look at the billboards, open a glossy magazine or pay attention to social media and you'll see instantly how powerful and persuasive they can be. What good is it to be successful, beautiful, fashionable and fit, if our humanity is lacking?

Imagine going into a shop to buy new clothes, cosmetics or fitness gear and asking if you can get an order of kindness or a side of compassion with that?

Imagine being able to find caring, kindness, generosity and humility as easily as we find the other.

Imagine if companies with massive advertising budgets found kindness and human warmth to be important?

Imagine the change if kindness was presented as desirable.

What if kindness was offered as a requirement in school? A credit course taught on consideration.

We don't need to shut down the Internet or turn off the Television. We don't need to restrict content or intent but we do need a balance.

If kindness is ever to succeed it must be offered as a clear, exciting option.

An Easier Life

Sometimes the most important things are those that are the most obvious. Some go to great lengths to find "the answers" and "the secrets" of life. Sometimes we need to make things complicated. When the quest has mystery and drama the appeal goes up. If there's the sense something is hidden or being protected, the lure is high and we become convinced the most worthwhile things need to be searched for.

Religions like to do this. They speak of mysteries or things not yet revealed. They enjoy keeping people searching and guessing. They like you to believe there's more. You just need to look harder, try harder and be more faithful, then you'll finally understand.

I'm reminded of a time I went to an art gallery to view the works of a master painter. The woman on my right had a headset on and stood in front of the painting I was looking at. When she went to move away, I asked her what she had learned. She took off the device and told me the history of the painting, the mood of the artist that day, his psychological profile, the meaning of every bend and shape, the precise reason why he'd chosen the colours that were presented and so much more, I lost my focus.

I recall standing there dumbfounded when a younger woman who had been standing on my other side came closer to say, "maybe he just wanted to paint some flowers".

In my mind, the younger woman had it right. There was no mystery needed or profile required. All that mattered was the beauty of the painting. Anymore seemed to muddy the water and take away from what I can only imagine the painter intended.

So often we make a mess of the simple things. The flowers in the gallery reminded me, that long explanations and over-examination can have us miss the point. Now all I could do was hear the person under the headphones. The flowers were gone. I didn't want to look any more. I was lost.

We cannot, nor will we ever understand love in the context of relating to those we do not know how to love. Love is special. It's for family; for our children, our parents, our lovers and close friends who have gained that status over long periods of time and through many experiences shared.

Expect me to love those I become close to and those I associate with in special ways. Encourage me to love those I make commitments to and those I become intimately involved with; this I understand. This is part of my training and my conditioning and this makes sense.

Tell me to love those I barely know or those I don't know at all. Tell me to love those I don't care for or even those who are considered "my enemies" and it all gets lost. Like the painting at the art gallery, I'm now so confused I just want to move on and forget the whole thing.

I have no idea what love means outside the context I have spent years being taught, and because of that I can't make sense of applying love in places where it doesn't fit.

It's not love that will fix us, help us or change the world, because relative to our training, love doesn't make sense and therefore it doesn't work.

We crave change. We speak of doing things differently. We ask for justice, fairness and peace. We speak equity, equality and we long for things to be new and hopeful. Unfortunately, we don't have a framework or a point of reference because the songs and the poems, the scriptures, placards and posters are all confusing and misleading.

The answer to all the searching and struggling isn't love it's kindness. Kindness is a reference we all understand. There is no secret or mystery.

Kindness provides us with a framework we can comprehend and with a plan everyone can relate to. We all "get it and know it" because it makes sense and we know what it feels like.

We don't need headphones to appreciate beauty and we don't need complicated instruction to be kind. We get to care for each other. We get to be nice, patient, thoughtful, warm, considerate and compassionate. These are things each of us understands and things each of us recognizes we need.

I can be kind to you without having to love you.

I can be kind without having to make a huge commitment.

I can be kind without needing a guide or an interpreter.

I can be kind and in doing so I fix the majority of the world's problems and I heal myself. Now, I have purpose and meaning and it all makes sense.

We are experts in understanding the world. We live it every day. We all know what works, what's needed and what's lacking.

Why bother to be kind you might ask? Because it's simple, understandable and what we search for.

We must learn to tell each other what we need and find a way to hear what's being said.

"I heard you and I know how to respond."

"I know how to do that because it's exactly what I need too. Kindness."

Each time you reach out, each time you leave your needs behind and get out of yourself long enough to see there are others too, others in need, others you can make a difference for, you help yourself.

Each time you give you are honestly and humbly richer. Your caring, even for a moment, will provide you with a rich experience and an intangible bit of humanity that's impossible to gather anywhere else. See what unselfish, caring and kindness feel like and then you'll see while you're being a considerate person, you're also rewarded beyond anything you may have felt before.

It's here, in the act of being kind to others where we meet that "fix the world, help the world" thing face to face. They beg us, ask us, pray for us, chant to us, to love and change the world.

This is where we can make life easier. By choosing to be kind, we recognize that the world and those in it are in need of a warm response. Our kind, generous, compassionate acts will take some of life's pressures off those we interact with and we will begin to move away from being consumed with the ongoing worry and pre-occupation of our own lives.

The world will change by kindness because kindness is tangible, understandable and within our grasp every moment.

Brutal, arrogant, pushy and self-centered don't work. We've seen and experienced that and go on feeling and seeing it every day. Those qualities and others like them only encourage more of the same and we don't need that anymore. We must recognize our humanity in order to realize we require a fix. Not more of the same but a true response to a "hungry world".

Kindness isn't new but it is exciting and unusual. Kindness doesn't need interpretation and it actually makes a difference. Imagine if we were all just a little kinder how the shift would be felt everywhere. The pictures are astounding, the change immediate.

Act out of kindness because it makes sense and offers new possibilities. Your kindness will allow others to grow and thrive. It will allow them to trip and fall in the safety of your permission. It will offer a sense of caring unknown before and provide the excitement to go on risking, experimenting and learning.

Offer more than you hope to receive. Your kindness will appreciate my fragility and you will care for me regardless. Your Kindness will recognize my humanity and respond to its delicate nature. It will grasp my flawed nature and allow my imperfections in the name of a better tomorrow and another attempt. It will offer me options I did not know existed.

Your ability to be kind helps others with the burden of their lives and in the process, you give up the non-stop concern of being you.

When you experience kindness from another for no other reason than they are happy to offer it, you will be touched by the spirit of new and different and you will know so much more is possible.

May I always remember to be kind.

john martin is the author of *I Can't Stop Crying, Grief and Recovery a Compassionate Guide; The Damaged Child, A Handbook for Kindness and Hope and Help Me I Hurt*. He is also a contributor to *I Don't Know What to Say, How to Help and Support Someone Who is Dying* by Dr. Robert Buckman.

www.ingramcontent.com/pod-product-compliance
Lightning Source LLC
Chambersburg PA
CBHW060950050726
47592CB00003B/1178